COUNCIL on FOREIGN RELATIONS

Annual Report 2021

Annual Report
July 1, 2020–June 30, 2021

Council on Foreign Relations

58 East 68th Street
New York, NY 10065
tel 212.434.9400

1777 F Street, NW
Washington, DC 20006
tel 202.509.8400

cfr.org
communications@cfr.org

Contents

Mission Statement

The Council on Foreign Relations (CFR) is an independent, nonpartisan membership organization, think tank, and publisher dedicated to being a resource for its members, government officials, business executives, journalists, educators and students, civic and religious leaders, and other interested citizens in order to help them better understand the world and the foreign policy choices facing the United States and other countries.

Founded in 1921, CFR takes no institutional positions on matters of policy. CFR carries out its mission by

- maintaining a diverse membership, including special programs to promote interest and develop expertise in the next generation of foreign policy leaders;
- convening meetings at its headquarters in New York and in Washington, DC, and other cities where senior government officials, members of Congress, global leaders, and prominent thinkers come together with CFR members to discuss and debate major international issues;
- supporting a Studies Program that fosters independent research, enabling CFR scholars to produce articles, reports, and books and hold roundtables that analyze foreign policy issues and make concrete policy recommendations;
- publishing *Foreign Affairs*, the preeminent journal of international affairs and U.S. foreign policy;
- sponsoring Independent Task Forces that produce reports with both findings and policy prescriptions on the most important foreign policy topics; and
- providing up-to-date information and analysis about world events and American foreign policy on its website, CFR.org.

Letter From the Chair

Chairman
David M. Rubenstein

This was an extraordinary year for the Council. Established in the wake of a global pandemic of influenza, CFR experienced its centennial year amid another—COVID-19. Although the celebrations this year could not be in person, CFR marked the occasion with a special website, a new CFR store, dedicated programming, and a short history book.

One hundred years ago, an intense debate about America's role in the world gripped the nation, and isolationism and a form of America First ideologies enjoyed widespread support. The Senate dashed President Woodrow Wilson's hopes that the United States would join and lead the League of Nations, but a small group of business and civic leaders took up the mantle and formed a new organization dedicated to U.S. foreign policy and international relations. Many had been members of what was called the Inquiry, a group of men who accompanied Wilson as experts during the Paris Peace Conference. In its wake, they created a nonpartisan organization with an invitation-only membership: the Council on Foreign Relations. Early members launched study groups, meetings, and dinner discussions with academics, statesmen, and business leaders. They focused on exerting behind-the-scenes influence designed to encourage sustained U.S. involvement in the world.

As time progressed and the United States and the world were buffeted by economic disruption and a drift toward what became a second world war, the Council provided invaluable expertise and solidified its role as the most influential foreign policy institution in the world. Its magazine, *Foreign Affairs*, was launched in 1922 and quickly became the premier publication in the field. When the United States entered World War II in 1941, the Council helped policymakers grapple with both wartime considerations and plans for the postwar global order through its specially commissioned War and Peace Studies project. The Council helped shape the policy debate as the world entered the Cold War, first by publishing George F. Kennan's famous "X" article, "Sources of Soviet Conduct," then by helping lay the groundwork for U.S. nuclear policy by publishing a best-selling book, *Nuclear Weapons and Foreign Policy*, based on a CFR study group led by a young Henry A. Kissinger.

Vice Chairman
Blair Effron

Vice Chairman
Jami Miscik

As the Cold War continued, debate over the Vietnam War eroded the consensus on U.S. foreign policy that had developed during the Second World War and informed the early years of the Cold War. The Council itself was weakened given these divisions. Chairman David Rockefeller ushered in a new era. The organization began to modernize, bringing in younger members and in 1970 finally admitting women.

Nonetheless, the Council faced a difficult few decades as foreign policy became more broadly debated. Think tanks proliferated; the media landscape changed. As the Cold War was ending, two leaders made a real difference and put the Council back at the forefront: Leslie H. Gelb and Richard N. Haass. Gelb worked to expand the membership base, bringing in younger and more diverse people, launching task forces, and expanding CFR's role in the media. Haass continued on that path, revitalizing and broadening the scope of the David Rockefeller Studies Program, creating a significant digital presence, and greatly expanding the Council's role as an educator for members and nonmembers alike in and out of classrooms. In so doing, the Council rebooted its reputation and influence. A new book released this year by George Gavrilis, *The Council on Foreign Relations: A Short History*, recounts all this in much greater detail and is well worth a read. It can be found on the Council's centennial website, cfr.org/100, highlights from which are included in a special section of this annual report.

As CFR's history demonstrates, the membership component of the Council makes it unique among think thanks. The trajectory of membership says something about the changes taking place in the United States. What began in 1921 as a group made up mostly of white, northeastern men, the Council now boasts more than five thousand members, a racially and ethnically diverse group of women and men from all over the country and with a broad range of backgrounds and expertise. Members have included seven U.S. presidents, thirty-seven secretaries of state, twenty-two secretaries of defense, twenty-five secretaries of the treasury, twenty-one national security advisors, six Supreme Court justices, and twenty-four Nobel Prize winners. A graphic depiction of this growth and change is featured on the centennial website and later in this report that shows a sample of the impressive people who have been members and how the membership has come to much better reflect society writ large. That said, much work is still to be done, and the Council will continue on a path toward making its twenty-first-century membership much more representative and diverse.

As the Council prepared to mark its centennial, everything changed as the country and the world clamped down to combat a global pandemic. Fortunately, the Council was well prepared and rose to the occasion to serve the membership and continue its mission. A shift to virtual events meant opportunities for speakers and members to participate regardless of location. World leaders such as Ashraf Ghani of Afghanistan, Jacinda Ardern of New Zealand, and Sebastian Pinera of Chile met with members; meanwhile, the Council continued to bring together the best and most authoritative experts to cover subjects such as climate change, infectious disease, democratic backsliding, cybersecurity, and the growing rivalry between the United States and both China and Russia. Participation by members and others has been higher than ever before.

The Council issued two important reports this year by Independent Task Forces, one on China's Belt and Road Initiative and the other on improving pandemic preparedness. Scholars in the David Rockefeller Studies Program published eight books. At the same time, fellows produced more than twenty reports and more than five hundred articles and op-eds, and the department convened more than two hundred and fifty roundtable meetings. Traffic on CFR.org, ForeignAffairs.com, and the newest website, Think Global Health, reached record levels. On the education front, the number of users for both the World101 program, CFR's online modular course focused on fundamental concepts of international relations and foreign policy, and the Model Diplomacy program, CFR's National Security Council and UN Security Council simulation program, grew markedly, as has the quantity of content both programs offer. Outreach to constituencies such as state and local officials and religious leaders increased in scope and continued to garner participation rates far above prepandemic levels. All of this is to say that CFR not only weathered the storm of COVID-19 but also exceeded expectations—and did so in a way true to its principles of nonpartisanship and independence.

In many ways, the Council finds itself in a similar landscape to that of its founding: a global pandemic, trends of isolationism and America First, and continued crises across the world. But the Council's ability to tackle the issues of the day while seamlessly pivoting to remote work goes to show the strength of foundation the institution developed over the last hundred years. Richard Haass's strong and steady leadership has been invaluable in helping guide the organization through these extraordinary circumstances; many thanks as well go to the Council staff, my fellow members of the Board of Directors, and the Council's membership. The Council has remained well positioned to continue to operate at a fast pace and a high level in challenging circumstances. I am confident this will not change. The Council will continue to fulfill its mission to help its members, government officials, business executives, journalists, and other interested citizens better understand the world and the foreign policy choices facing the United States, as it has done for a century now. As Richard's essay makes clear, the challenges facing the country and the world in the twenty-first century are considerable, and we are fortunate to have an organization well positioned to take them on and help guide us through the complicated times to come.

President's Message

President
Richard N. Haass

History is the study of the past, but the Council's principal task is to try to make sense of the present and future, an undertaking that is often assisted by discerning and applying lessons derived from the past. Such help is welcome, as the world that is unfolding three-quarters of a century after the end of World War II and three decades after the end of the Cold War, the world that will form the backdrop to CFR's second century, is as dynamic as it is complex.

One central characteristic of today's world is the revival of great power rivalry. But even describing it as a revival obscures some basic truths. The challenge China poses to the United States and the international system is fundamentally different than anything seen before given the scale and reach of its economy. It is impossible to contain a country so integrated in the world, one that maintains close trade and investment relationships with many of the United States' closest security partners. It is also why analogies to the Cold War are misplaced. One of the major foreign policy challenges facing the United States will be how to structure an increasingly competitive political and economic relationship with China, one also defined by profound differences in their domestic and foreign policy agendas, so that it does not spill over into armed confrontation or preclude cooperation where it would serve both countries' interests.

Russia represents an entirely different kind of great power challenge. It is familiar and formidable alike. Vladimir Putin's Russia is not particularly interested in economic integration, which it sees as a potential threat to its repressive political system and leadership. What it is willing to do is use its military power, energy resources, and cyber tools to advance its overseas interests. Here too the challenge for the United States is to deter or defend against destabilizing Russian behavior without triggering direct confrontation or ruling out the possibility of limited cooperation in areas such as nuclear arms control.

It is also important to note that in today's world a country need not qualify as a great power to have great impact in its region or on occasion beyond. Today's world is one of dispersed power. Yet it is also one of widespread national weakness, of governments unable to fulfill their basic obligation to provide security to their citizens and regulate what happens within their borders.

As if all this were not enough, it is quite possible that this century will be defined less by geopolitics than by the willingness (or lack of it) of governments to pool their resources to meet the myriad challenges produced by globalization and the vast, fast flows across borders of just about everything, from greenhouse gases warming the planet to infectious diseases. The supply of vaccines with the potential to protect against COVID-19 and its variants is woefully inadequate. The number of refugees and internally displaced persons is at a historic high. Cyberspace is essentially unregulated. Supply chains have been shown to lack resilience. These and other examples make clear that globalization is winning the race over global governance.

All this and more is playing out in a context defined by a third factor: the emergence of a United States increasingly preoccupied with domestic matters, yet so divided politically that any consensus on what to do about them is nearly impossible. These same divisions have carried over to much of foreign policy, with the result that there is no agreement on American priorities in the world or how to achieve them. It also turns out the United States is no more immune to democratic backsliding than are others, a reality that further works against its ability to present an attractive model that others will want to emulate.

Here at CFR, we plan to address these and related issues in three main ways. The first is to do what we have always done: provide policy-relevant material—background, analysis, policy choices—to our members, policymakers in the executive branch and Congress, the media, and business leaders. We will regularly offer a forum for meetings and discussion and debate for heads of state and government, senior government officials, members of Congress, and a broad range of experts. CFR scholars will analyze pressing global challenges and propose how they can best be addressed in their books, articles, discussion papers, policy briefs, reports, op-eds, and podcasts. *Foreign Affairs* will remain the premier venue in the world for thoughtful, in-depth treatment of national security and global challenges.

The second is to reach out to broader segments of the population to help encourage a more informed citizenry. CFR will continue to educate and inform nonmembers who traditionally have been peripherally involved in foreign policy discussions, including congregational and religious leaders, state and local officials, local journalists, students and teachers, and other citizens. This will be done through meetings, roundtables, webinar series, workshops, briefings, and material developed for and posted on CFR.org. The Council's education initiative, including the Model Diplomacy and World101 programs, will be a resource for students to become globally literate and develop the necessary background to prepare for a wide range of careers.

Third, CFR will help develop the next generation of foreign policy leaders by creating and strengthening talent pipelines that draw on and reflect our diverse society. Our more recent efforts include the expansion of the internship program, which provides an opportunity for students from all over the country to work at CFR and participate in professional development workshops. Junior staffers are involved in CFR work and privy to meetings and development workshops akin to those offered to the interns. As with interns and junior staff, CFR senior staff and fellows go on to positions of influence in government, academia, business, and the media. CFR also maintains multiple fellowship programs including the International Affairs Fellowship, Military Fellowship program, the Edward R. Murrow Press Fellowship, and the National Intelligence Fellowship. Outside of fellowships, young professionals can join CFR through the Stephen M. Kellen Term Member Program. For those in more established positions later in their careers, CFR offers the life membership program. The aim will be to expand those efforts and foster talent so that the leaders of tomorrow better reflect our society and are better able to contend with the foreign policy challenges sure to face the country.

Had the Inquiry of 1918 not led to the founding of CFR in 1921, as depicted by David Rubenstein in his essay, what is described here would make a strong case for founding CFR today. Thankfully, it does exist, and there is no shortage of issues to keep the Council occupied for the next hundred years. This work is all made possible with the support of the Board of Directors and the Global Board of Advisors. CFR members for their part do so much to enrich our output and further our mission with their involvement in and commitment to the institution. Finally, we could not succeed without the dedication and professionalism of our staff. As it begins its second hundred years, CFR will continue to serve an ever-broadening audience with smart, independent, policy-relevant but nonpartisan research and analysis to help create a better understanding of the foreign policy challenges facing this country and the choices for addressing them.

Richard N. Haass
President

2021 Highlights

The COVID-19 pandemic continued over the last year, but the Council on Foreign Relations rose to the challenge. These highlights reflect a year of entirely virtual operations.

Meetings

The Council on Foreign Relations provides a nonpartisan forum for thoughtful and informed foreign policy debate, drawing leaders and experts in government, business, the media, and academia for discussions with members on critical issues in foreign policy and international relations.

Although in-person meetings were not possible during the opening of the UN General Assembly in the fall—traditionally the busiest time of year for CFR in New York—CFR did host virtual events with a number of heads of state and foreign ministers, including Afghanistan Chairman of the High Council for National Reconciliation Abdullah Abdullah, United Arab Emirates (UAE) Foreign Minister Abdullah bin Zayed Al Nahyan, New Zealand Prime Minister Jacinda Ardern, Israeli Foreign Minister Gabi Ashkenazi, President of Colombia Ivan Duque, UAE Minister of State Anwar Gargash, Afghanistan President Ashraf Ghani, Foreign Minister A. K. Abdul Momen of Bangladesh, President Sebastian Pinera of Chile, Prime Minister Mohammad Shtayyeh of the Palestinian Authority, President Ursula von der Leyen of the European Commission, State Councilor and Foreign Minister Wang Yi of China, and Foreign Minister of Iran Javad Zarif.

Current and former U.S. officials also spoke at CFR. During the final months of the Donald Trump administration, members heard from U.S. Special Representative for Venezuela Elliott Abrams, U.S. International Development Finance Corporation CEO Adam Boehler, Director of the National Institute of Allergy and Infectious Diseases Anthony S. Fauci, Special Representative for Iran Brian Hook, U.S. Trade Representative Robert Lighthizer, National Economic Council Director Larry Kudlow, Centers for Disease Control and Prevention Director Robert Redfield, Export-Import Bank Chairman Kimberly Reed, and Director of the National Geospatial-Intelligence Agency Robert Sharp. Other officials who spoke to members virtually include World Food Program Director David Beasley, Representatives Ami Bera (D-CA) and James Clyburn (D-SC), former U.S. Secretary of Defense Robert Gates, former World Bank President Robert Zoellick, as well as former Secretaries of State Hillary Clinton and Henry A. Kissinger.

To round out CFR's Election 2020 series, CFR held two virtual forums in October, hosting more than 1,600 participants at each. These nonpartisan events, open to the general public and members alike, featured conversations on foreign policy challenges awaiting the winner of the 2020 presidential election. In early 2021, CFR launched the Transition 2021 meeting series examining foreign policy challenges facing the Joe Biden administration. Sessions addressed topics that included Afghanistan, China, domestic terrorism and post-insurrection, Latin America and the Caribbean, North Korea, the Israeli-Palestinian conflict, Russia, South Asia and geopolitical competition, U.S.-Europe relations and prospects for transatlantic cooperation, U.S.-Iran relations, and U.S.-Saudi relations. CFR also instituted another new speaker series in connection with its centennial with leading thinkers tackling issues that will define this century. Speakers thus far have included Margaret MacMillan on what history has to tell us, Anne Applebaum on democracy, and Nicholas Stern on climate change.

CFR's CEO speaker series included Alex Gorsky of Johnson & Johnson, Scott Kirby of United Airlines, Martin Sorrell of S4 Capital, Kathy Warden of Northrop Grumman, and Bill Winters of Standard Chartered Bank. Mastercard Executive Chairman Ajay Banga also spoke for this year's Bernard L. Schwartz Lecture on Economic Growth and Foreign Policy. As part of CFR's C. Peter McColough Series on International Economics, members heard from Federal Reserve Bank of Atlanta President and

***Top:** Chinese State Councilor Wang Yi discusses China's foreign and domestic policies, including the effects of COVID-19 and the future of U.S.-China relations.*

***Bottom:** President of the European Commission Ursula von der Leyen discusses her vision for a new transatlantic agenda and the future of multilateralism.*

Chairman and CEO of Johnson & Johnson Alex Gorsky discusses COVID-19 vaccine development and lessons learned throughout his career with Executive Chairman and CEO of Cerevel Therapeutics and CFR Board member Tony Coles.

CEO Raphael Bostic, Federal Reserve Member Lael Brainard, Vice Chairman of the Federal Reserve Richard Clarida, International Monetary Fund Managing Director Kristalina Georgieva, Federal Reserve Bank of Dallas Chair Robert Kaplan, World Bank President David Malpass, and former Treasury Secretary Lawrence Summers. Additionally, this year the Stephen C. Freidheim Symposium on Global Economics focused on the global economy amid the pandemic and featured former Governor of the Bank of England and Bank of Canada Mark Carney.

CFR also hosted several symposia this spring that took a deeper dive into various topics. This year's Rita Hauser Annual Event, featuring keynote speaker Larry Fink of BlackRock, addressed the financial risks of climate change. The Robert B. Menschel Economics Symposium, featuring keynote speaker Richard H. Thaler, focused on behavioral economics during the pandemic. The Ending Human Trafficking in the Twenty-First Century Symposium, featuring keynote speaker Guy Ryder, focused on the economic costs of forced labor and the role of governments and the public sector in combating human trafficking. Additional symposia covered the cybersecurity threat from Russia and the outlook for U.S. policy toward Taiwan.

This year marked the fiftieth anniversary of the Stephen M. Kellen Term Member Program. The anniversary was celebrated during the annual conference, held in October 2020, which included keynote conversations with former U.S. Secretary of State (and former term member) John Kerry and former U.S. National Security Advisor H. R. McMaster. Other events focused on the COVID-19 pandemic from the perspective of frontline workers, the importance of diversity in national security, China's Belt and Road Initiative, and how the pandemic affected emerging markets. Term members also had the opportunity to meet at monthly Zoom happy hours.

In May, CFR convened the Conference on Diversity in International Affairs. The annual event, a collaborative effort by CFR, the Global Access Pipeline, and the International Career Advancement Program, brought together more than three hundred participants from diverse racial, ethnic, and socioeconomic backgrounds that are historically underrepresented in the field of foreign policy. This was the ninth diversity conference and featured a conversation with Ford Foundation President Darren Walker.

National Program

The National Program connects the plurality of CFR members who live outside New York and Washington, DC, with CFR and its resources. Virtual programming this year allowed members to participate in interactive roundtables via Zoom and gave them unprecedented access to CFR's regular meetings series.

In December 2020, CFR convened the sixth annual National Symposium. This year's online format made it possible for more than four hundred members from around the country and abroad to attend—more than double the level of previous in-person participation. The symposium included conversations on U.S. foreign policy in the wake of the pandemic, the climate crisis, and COVID-19 vaccines.

CFR's annual National Conference in June was also held virtually, with New Zealand Prime Minister Jacinda Ardern speaking from Auckland for the keynote session. The conference included a discussion on the U.S. response to China's Belt and Road Initiative, a talk on how to bridge the political divide in the United States, and a panel featuring several members of CFR's Global Board of Advisors on the world after COVID-19. Board Chair David Rubenstein and CFR President Richard Haass closed the conference with a town hall discussion on CFR at one hundred, looking back at its history and what lies ahead.

CFR President Richard N. Haass speaks with Prime Minister of New Zealand Jacinda Ardern on the country's response to COVID-19 and leadership on a global stage, at the opening of CFR's National Conference.

New York Times *reporter and editorial board member Farah Stockman and Distinguished Fellow Martin S. Indyk speak at a roundtable with national members on escalating tensions in the Israeli-Palestinian conflict.*

Clockwise from top left: *President and CEO of Softtek Blanca Trevino, Senior Partner at McKinsey & Company and CFR Board member James Manyika, Founder and Executive Chairman of Econet Group and CFR's Global Board of Advisors (GBA) member Strive Masiyiwa, Founder and Chairman of Bharti Enterprises and GBA member Sunil Bharti Mittal, and Founder and Chairman of the Mo Ibrahim Foundation and GBA member Mo Ibrahim discuss global perspectives on the world after COVID-19.*

Corporate Program

CFR's Corporate Program provides member companies from across the globe access to CFR experts, research, and meetings to help them better understand the international issues that affect their businesses. This year, the program held roundtables on issues including U.S. trade policy, climate pressures on energy markets, sustainable finance, and the risk of inflation. Other meetings covered the topics of central bank digital currencies, the balkanization of the internet, vaccine inequality, and racial inequity in the private sector.

The annual Corporate Conference was held virtually in 2021, featuring a keynote conversation with Alphabet and Google Chief Financial Officer Ruth Porat as well as sessions on geopolitical risk, the global economy, and the world's recovery from the COVID-19 pandemic. CFR hosted its third annual CEO Summit in June, bringing together thirty-three leading executives for a candid discussion on many of the economic, geopolitical, and societal factors affecting the private sector.

Clockwise from top left: *Global economist Dambisa Moyo, Chair of the Mastercard Impact Fund Martina Hund-Mejean, and Distinguished Professor of the Graduate School at the Haas School of Business at University of California, Berkeley, Laura D. Tyson discuss the relationship between markets and society at the Corporate Program's "Future of Capitalism" roundtable.*

The David Rockefeller Studies Program

The Studies Program, CFR's think tank, analyzes pressing global challenges and offers recommendations for policymakers in the United States and elsewhere. CFR's research aims to be more policy relevant than that of most universities and more rigorous than what many advocacy groups produce.

CFR experts published eight books this year. Books reflect the emphasis CFR places on in-depth research and analysis. Mira Rapp-Hooper's book *An Open World: How America Can Win the Contest for Twenty-First-Century Order*, coauthored with Rebecca Lissner, argues that the days of U.S. primacy have passed and that the United States can best protect and advance its national interests by renovating existing international institutions and creating new ones. In *Losing the Long Game: The False Promise of Regime Change in the Middle East*, Senior Fellow Philip H. Gordon points out that regime change efforts in the Middle East have proved far more costly and less beneficial than initially predicted and that a combination of containment, deterrence, and diplomacy would be a better approach. In *Toxic Politics: China's Environmental Health Crisis and Its Challenge to the Chinese State*, Senior Fellow Yanzhong Huang assesses the consequences of China's environmental degradation on its economy, politics, and society. In *Isolationism: A History of America's Efforts to Shield Itself From the World*, Senior Fellow Charles A. Kupchan advocates for a judicious retrenchment to bring the nation's commitments back into line with its purposes and means.

Senior Fellow John Campbell's book *Nigeria and the Nation-State: Rethinking Diplomacy With the Postcolonial World* provides insights into the prospects and pitfalls facing Africa's most populous country and calls on the United States to refocus its bilateral relationship beyond Nigeria's national government. Senior Fellow Ray Takeyh's *The Last Shah: America, Iran, and the Fall of the Pahlavi Dynasty* argues that the 1979 Iranian Revolution was the product of decades of erosion of Iran's political establishment under a monarch who lacked the personal strength to make hard decisions and ultimately lost the support of every sector of Iranian society. Adjunct Senior Fellow Gayle Tzemach Lemmon's *The Daughters of Kobani: A Story of Rebellion, Courage, and Justice* draws on hundreds of hours of interviews and on-the-ground reporting to tell the story of the all-female Kurdish militia against the self-proclaimed Islamic State in northeastern Syria. Adjunct Senior Fellow Stephen Biddle's *Nonstate Warfare: The Military Methods of Guerillas, Warlords, and Militias* observes that, rather than pursuing a different style of warfare, many nonstate actors in fact adopt more conventional battle tactics than state armies do.

In Council Special Reports, CFR experts provide timely responses to developing crises and contribute to policy dilemmas. CFR published five in the last year. In *The Day After in Venezuela: Delivering Security and Dispensing Justice*, Fellow Paul J. Angelo maintains that the United States should begin planning now for the possible end of the Nicolas Maduro presidency and thereby help facilitate Venezuela's return to democracy. Senior Fellow Robert K. Knake's *Weaponizing Digital Trade: Creating a Digital Trade Zone to Promote Online Freedom and Cybersecurity* recommends that the United States and its allies create a digital trade zone of common standards and practices that excludes those countries that do not abide by those standards. In *Revitalizing the State Department and American Diplomacy*, Adjunct Senior Fellow Jon Finer and Alliance for Peacebuilding President Uzra Zeya contend that the Department of State has fallen into a deep and sustained crisis. They call for an ambitious departmental

Clockwise from top left: *Director of National Security and Professor of Strategic Studies at the Marine Corps War College Tammy S. Schultz, Adjunct Senior Fellow Gayle Tzemach Lemmon, and Senior Fellow Max Boot discuss the Joe Biden administration's decision to withdraw all troops from Afghanistan by September 2021.*

reform effort to stem talent flight and remedy deficiencies in policymaking and capacity. In *The United States, China, and Taiwan: A Strategy to Prevent War*, Senior Fellow Robert D. Blackwill and University of Virginia Professor Philip Zelikow argue that the threat of war over Taiwan is becoming the world's most dangerous flash point and recommend the United States not only cease unnecessary provocations and clarify that it is not trying to change Taiwan's status but also prepare new plans that could challenge Chinese actions and help Taiwan defend itself, yet put the burden of widening a war on China. They also posit that the United States should closely coordinate U.S.-Taiwan policy with Japan and other Asian allies and should conclude a bilateral trade agreement with Taiwan. In *Ending Human Trafficking in the Twenty-First Century*, Senior Fellows Jamille Bigio and Rachel B. Vogelstein urge the United States to increase investment in anti-trafficking measures as a matter of national security.

The Center for Preventive Action, under the direction of Senior Fellow Paul B. Stares, published the thirteenth annual *Preventive Priorities Survey*. Five hundred foreign policy experts evaluated which conflicts around the world could escalate and harm U.S. interests in 2021. Their top concerns include North Korea's further development of nuclear weapons and ballistic missiles, increasing violence and political instability in Afghanistan, and the ongoing reimposition of government control in Syria.

The Diamonstein-Spielvogel Project on the Future of Democracy was launched this year with a generous grant from the Diamonstein-Spielvogel Foundation to identify threats to the health of democracies around the world and outline steps to reverse the erosion of democratic norms and values. CFR also rebooted the Renewing America initiative, which shines a spotlight on the domestic underpinnings of U.S. competitiveness to find ways to bolster U.S. international strength and influence. CFR fellows continued work in response to COVID-19, producing more than 20 reports and roughly 530 articles and op-eds, and convened more than 250 roundtable meetings on a wide range of topics, including the Israeli-Palestinian conflict, Afghanistan, and domestic terrorism.

Member of the Federal Reserve System Board of Governors Lael Brainard discusses the challenges facing U.S. economic recovery with President and CEO of TIAA Roger W. Ferguson Jr. as part of the C. Peter McColough Series on International Economics.

The think tank welcomed several new full-time and adjunct fellows this year. Elliott Abrams returned to CFR as a senior fellow, Luciana Borio and Jennifer Nuzzo both joined as senior fellows for global health, Heidi Crebo-Rediker returned as an adjunct fellow, Roger W. Ferguson Jr. joined as the Steven A. Tananbaum distinguished fellow for international economics, Brent McIntosh joined as an adjunct senior fellow for international economics and finance, Yascha Mounk joined as a senior fellow, Justin Muzinich joined as a distinguished fellow, and Gideon Rose returned to the Studies Program from *Foreign Affairs* as a distinguished fellow.

Senior Fellow Yanzhong Huang discusses his new CFR Book, Toxic Politics: China's Environmental Health Crisis and Its Challenge to the Chinese State, *with CFR President Richard Haass.*

Council of Councils

This year, the Council of Councils, a consortium of twenty-eight leading think tanks from around the world that convenes semiannually to discuss the state of global governance and how to improve it, met in November and May. At the group's tenth annual conference in May, members discussed a wide range of topics on global governance, including the future of multilateralism, international cooperation on COVID-19 vaccines, nuclear proliferation, and global trade.

Task Forces

CFR's Independent Task Force Program convenes diverse and distinguished groups of experts who offer analysis of and policy prescriptions for major foreign policy issues facing the United States. The Task Force on Preparing for the Next Pandemic released its report, *Improving Pandemic Preparedness: Lessons From COVID-19*, in October 2020. Chaired by Board members Sylvia Mathews Burwell and Frances Fragos Townsend and directed by Senior Fellows Thomas J. Bollyky and Stewart M. Patrick, the Task Force proposes a comprehensive strategy including institutional reforms and policy innovations to help the United States and the multilateral system perform better in this crisis and when the next pandemic threat inevitably emerges. In March 2021, the Task Force on a U.S. Response to China's Belt and Road Initiative (BRI) released its report, *China's Belt and Road: Implications for the United States*. Chaired by former U.S. Treasury Secretary Jacob J. Lew and former Chief of Naval Operations Admiral Gary Roughead (retired) and directed by Senior Fellow Jennifer Hillman and Research Fellow David Sacks, the Task Force proposes that the United States should respond to the BRI with an affirmative agenda of its own, drawing on its strengths and coordinating with allies and partners to promote sustainable, secure, and green development around the world.

Clockwise from top left: *Task Force Codirector Stewart M. Patrick, host of NPR's* Weekend Edition Sunday *Lulu Garcia-Navarro, Task Force Codirector Thomas J. Bollyky, Task Force Co-chair Frances Fragos Townsend, and Task Force Co-chair Sylvia Mathews Burwell discuss the release of* Improving Pandemic Preparedness: Lessons From COVID-19.

Clockwise from the top left: *Task Force Codirector David Sacks, Task Force Co-chair Admiral Gary Roughead (Ret.), Task Force Codirector Jennifer Hillman, Task Force Co-chair Jacob J. Lew, and NPR host-at-large Elise Hu discuss the release of* China's Belt and Road: Implications for the United States.

Education

CFR's educational initiative aims to provide students with the skills and knowledge about the world to prepare them for a wide range of careers and to ensure an informed citizenry. Model Diplomacy, CFR's National Security Council and UN Security Council simulation program, continued to release new simulations and pop-up cases—short policy scenarios, some tied to current events and others to historical events. The COVID-19 response pop-up case was ranked in the top ten of partner lessons on Share My Lesson, a teaching resource website with 1.7 million members. Other cases focused on important foreign policy issues from U.S. history, including the Oregon boundary dispute of 1845 and influenza and war in 1918.

World101—CFR's online modular course that focuses on the fundamental concepts of international relations and foreign policy—continued to grow. The core World101 course was completed this year and offers four units: Global Era Issues, covering major global challenges such as climate change, nuclear proliferation, and terrorism; Regions of the World, exploring the major regions through lenses including history, economics, and U.S. foreign policy; How the World Works . . . and Sometimes Doesn't, covering topics such as sovereignty, nationalism, and global governance; and Historical Context, demonstrating what the past can teach about the present and future.

Partnerships and social media have been important drivers of growth. CFR has forged robust distribution partnerships with Nearpod, Newsela, SAFARI Montage, Share My Lesson, Composer, and three groups focused on civics education: Made By Us, Civics Unplugged, and CivXNow. Other partnerships include with the Gilder Lehrman Institute of American History to help amplify the release of the Historical Context unit and with the *New York Times* and the American Association of State Colleges and Universities (AASCU) that culminated in two student-centered Global Literacy Talks—sessions open to two million students on AASCU member campuses that feature facilitated group discussions based on World101 and *New York Times* materials.

Students at Lewis & Clark College take part in a Model Diplomacy simulation.

Outreach

Academic Outreach

CFR's Academic Outreach initiative connects educators and students with CFR publications, digital educational products, and programming for teaching and learning about international affairs. The Academic Webinar series provides a forum for the academic community to interact with CFR experts and other thought leaders and participate in foreign policy discussions. This year, webinars covered topics including isolationism, internationalism, and America's role in the world; European integration and Brexit; international trade policy; and the road to peace in Afghanistan.

The recently launched Higher Education Webinar series provides a forum for college and university leaders, administrators, and professors to explore strategic challenges and share best practices for meeting them. Topics this year included targeting, testing, and mitigating the spread of COVID-19; the value of international students; and planning for vaccine rollouts. CFR staff gave presentations on CFR academic resources at the Historically Black Colleges and Universities Faculty Development Network, the Community Colleges for International Development Annual Conference, and Stockton University's International Education Week. CFR's ninth annual College and University Educators Workshop featured panels on the president's foreign policy inbox, preparing for the future of work, and teaching with CFR resources. Finally, the *Academic Bulletin* remains a significant digital communication channel to showcase the breadth of resources and formats in CFR materials and has more than thirty thousand subscribers.

CFR provided briefings for the Global Kids Summer Institute, a program for underserved high school students that CFR has hosted in New York since 2006. Participants heard from CFR senior fellows on topics including isolationism, social movements for climate action, and the ways in which technology is enabling social progress globally.

Religion and Foreign Policy Program

Since 2006, CFR's Religion and Foreign Policy program has provided a unique nonpartisan forum in which to examine issues at the nexus of religion and U.S. foreign policy. The initiative aims to involve members of the religion community in foreign policy discussions, given the tremendous reach they have through weekly sermons, missionary trips, and educating the next generation of spiritual leaders.

In addition to the teleconference/webinar series that has been held since 2006, the program launched a second on Social Justice and Foreign Policy this year to explore the relationship between religion and social justice and its ramifications on foreign policy. Among the events was a conversation with Archbishop of New York Cardinal Timothy M. Dolan at the annual Religion and Foreign Policy Workshop. The program also continues to produce the monthly *Religion and Foreign Policy Bulletin*, which provides analysis of international issues of interest to the religion community and has more than twelve thousand subscribers.

Washington Outreach

CFR's Congress and U.S. Foreign Policy program aims to connect the work of CFR with members of Congress, their staffs, and executive branch officials. The program is an essential source of independent, nonpartisan analysis to inform the direction of U.S. foreign policy. It also offers a unique forum in which policymakers from both sides of the aisle can come together for all-too-rare reasoned discussions on foreign policy issues.

This year, the program facilitated briefings and consultations for Congress on virtual platforms and by telephone in addition to general outreach and relationship-building meetings with members of Congress and their staffs. Congress continues to turn to CFR for thoughtful analysis of the COVID-19 pandemic and CFR fellows have briefed members and staff from more than 250 offices. The program

Cardinal Timothy M. Dolan speaks with Religion News Service national reporter Jack Jenkins about how the Catholic church can help the United States further their shared foreign policy goals, as part of the Religion and Foreign Policy Workshop.

continues to host virtual events with embassies, including with ambassadors from Afghanistan, Australia, Brazil, Colombia, France, Singapore, and Spain, among other nations.

The House and Senate principals meeting series, cohosted with former Senator Tom Daschle and former Congressman Vin Weber, held roundtable conversations on the COVID-19 pandemic and on China. In March, the House and Senate principals meeting series held its first virtual roundtable of the 117th Congress, where twenty-three members of Congress joined Board member Meghan O'Sullivan and Richard Haass for a conversation on foreign policy. In light of the presidential transition, the program facilitated a number of consultations for incoming members of the Biden administration.

State and Local Outreach

CFR's State and Local Officials initiative connects governors, mayors, state legislators, and city and county leaders with resources on pressing global issues that affect local agendas. The initiative features a webinar series on international issues of local importance, showcases CFR experts at major gatherings of state and local leaders, and disseminates CFR publications to officials.

Interest in the program surged at the start of the pandemic, and attendance for the webinar series for this constituency remains high, with representation from every state and several U.S. territories over the course of the series. Sessions have featured discussions on election administration and mail-in voting with a panel of state-level secretaries of state and election experts, building broadband infrastructure, China's Belt and Road Initiative, countering extremism at the local level, and the American Rescue Plan and the CARES Act. Additionally, last summer, the program launched a monthly newsletter as a platform to regularly share CFR materials with officials; it now has ten thousand subscribers.

Local Journalists Initiative

To elevate conversations on U.S. foreign policy choices and increase civic participation, CFR's Local Journalists initiative helps native print, broadcast, and digital journalists working for regional outlets based across the United States to draw connections between the local issues they cover and national and international dynamics. CFR continued the conference call and webinar series for these journalists to connect them with experts and provide a forum for sharing best practices. On these calls, Adjunct Senior Fellow Carla Anne Robbins serves as host and is joined by experts and journalists who provide guidance for framing stories on topics such as COVID-19 vaccine distribution, misinformation campaigns, and racial health disparities. Over the last year, CFR has brought together nearly 350 journalists from across the country.

CFR Digital

CFR.org continues to be a leading source of timely analysis on critical foreign policy issues. The website's most popular content continues to be Backgrounders, which provide authoritative, accessible, and regularly updated primers on hundreds of foreign policy topics from around the globe, including the Iran nuclear deal and the Taliban. In Briefs provide succinct rundowns on important developments authored by CFR fellows and the CFR.org editorial team. Backgrounders and In Briefs this year covered topics that included comparing policing efforts worldwide, the U.S. withdrawal from Afghanistan, and the COVID-19 pandemic.

Throughout the presidential election, CFR.org's Election 2020 candidate position tracker, which offered an interactive guide to the differing foreign policy answers of the candidates, had tens of thousands of views. Other noteworthy content the editorial and digital teams published focused on the social justice protests sparked by the police killing of George Floyd, including CFR fellows assessing U.S. stature in the world and global policing efforts. Additionally, the Maurice R. Greenberg Center for Geoeconomic Studies launched a new interactive, the Global Growth Tracker, which charts the economic growth performance of ninety-one countries over the last twenty years.

Think Global Health, a multicontributor website that CFR launched in January 2020, explores how health challenges are reshaping economies, societies, and everyday lives around the world. It has produced more than 250 articles and received more than a million page views during its first year in operation.

Two CFR digital products were recognized for excellence with Webby nominations. The Think Global Health site was nominated in the Best Health and Wellness category, and a photo essay on CFR.org titled "Grieving in a Pandemic" was nominated in the category of Best Use of Photography.

CFR's public newsletters—including the *Daily News Brief* and *The World This Week*—continue to attract new subscribers. This year, CFR launched a new newsletter for members, *Members' Weekly*, to keep members informed about CFR updates and activities. In addition, CFR maintains a significant presence on social media. CFR institutional social media accounts have more than 420,000 likes on Facebook, 482,000 followers on Twitter, 193,000 on LinkedIn, and 30,000 on Instagram, reflecting steady growth on most channels. The CFR YouTube channel has more than 156,000 subscribers. CFR fellows have roughly 1.6 million followers on Twitter and 65,000 on Facebook.

COUNCIL *on* FOREIGN RELATIONS | 100

Foreign Affairs Newsletters

CFR Centennial Coronavirus Topics ▾ Regions ▾ Explainers ▾ Research & Analysis ▾ Communities ▾ Events ▾

A consequence of climate change is the increased likelihood of record-breaking floods. John Wark/Reuters

WRITTEN BY
Lindsay Maizland

UPDATED
Last updated April 29, 2021 12:00 pm (EST)

Introduction

What are the most important climate agreements?

Is there a consensus on the science?

Why is the 1.5°C goal so critical?

Which countries are responsible?

Is the Paris Agreement enough?

What are the alternatives to the Paris Agreement?

Recommended Resources

Summary

- Countries have debated how to combat climate change since the early 1990s. These negotiations have produced several important accords, including the Kyoto Protocol and the Paris Agreement.
- Governments generally agree on the science behind climate change but have diverged on who is most responsible and how to set emissions-reduction goals.
- Most experts say the Paris Agreement will not be enough to prevent the global average temperature from rising 1.5°C. If that happens, the world will suffer devastating consequences, such as heat waves and floods.

Introduction

Over the last several decades, governments have collectively pledged to slow global warming. But despite intensified diplomacy, the world could soon face devastating consequences of climate change.

RELATED

Envisioning a Green New Deal: A Global Comparison

by Andrew Chatzky *and* Anshu Siripurapu

Cyclone Idai Reveals Africa's Vulnerabilities

by Laura Hillard

CFR.org's newly designed Backgrounders display a more central feature photo, summary bullets, and an easy-to-navigate table of contents.

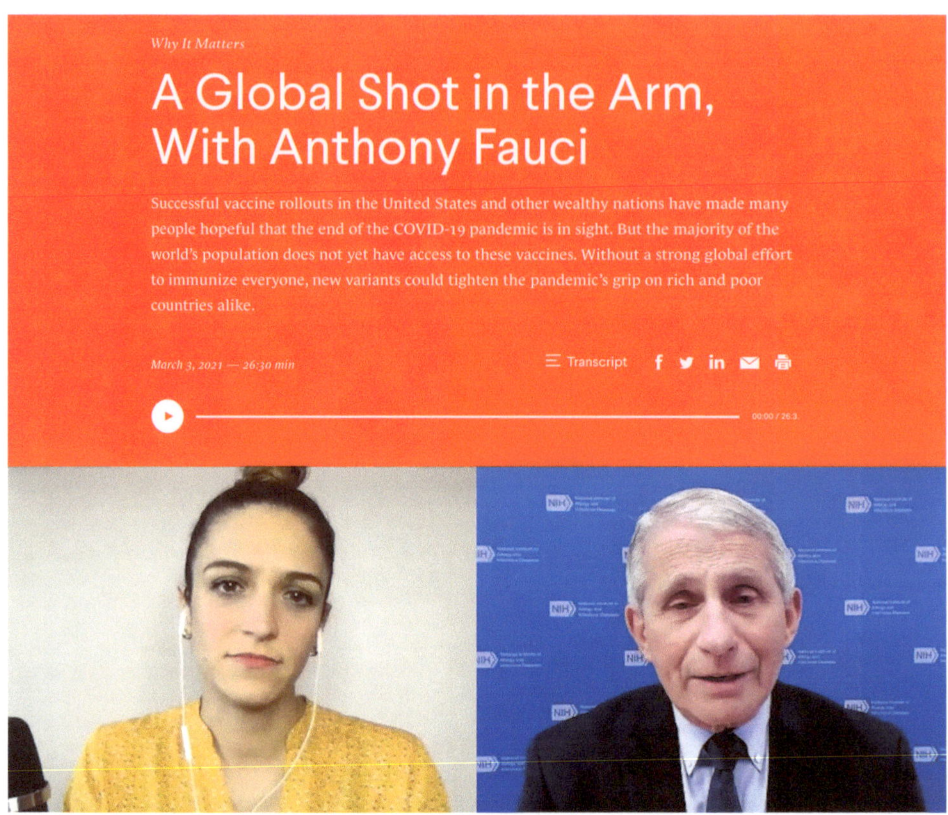

Top: *Host of the CFR podcast* Why It Matters *Gabrielle Sierra interviews Director of the National Institute of Allergy and Infectious Diseases Anthony S. Fauci on the global COVID-19 vaccine rollout.*

Bottom: *The online version of CFR's Independent Task Force report* China's Belt and Road: Implications for the United States *features direct quotes and critical takeaways in the executive summary.*

Foreign Affairs

Foreign Affairs magazine is the most thoughtful, read, and influential in its field. The magazine complements all else CFR does by providing a space for long-form analysis from a broad pool of expert voices. Each bimonthly print issue includes a lead package on a consequential issue, accompanied by comprehensive analysis of other challenges. In addition, ForeignAffairs.com offers in-depth commentary several times a week on the latest foreign policy developments.

This year saw a transition as Gideon Rose stepped down after a decade as editor to rejoin the David Rockefeller Studies Program and was succeeded by Daniel Kurtz-Phelan.

Lead packages in the magazine this year explored President Trump's legacy in foreign policy, vaccine nationalism, how to prepare for potential future catastrophes, the possibility of national renewal, foreign policy challenges facing the new administration, and trade and the global economy. The magazine also published contributions from former Secretary of State Hillary Clinton on a national security reckoning and from former Deputy Secretary of State William J. Burns and former Assistant Secretary of State for African Affairs Linda Thomas-Greenfield on the transformation of diplomacy, and included essays by former InterAmerican Development Bank President Luis Alberto Moreno on inequality in Latin America and former Chinese Communist Party official Cai Xia on the inner workings of Chinese power.

Highlights on ForeignAffairs.com included CFR's Thomas Bollyky and Chad P. Bown on global vaccine distribution, Ivo H. Daalder and CFR's James M. Lindsay on national security during presidential transitions, Michele A. Flournoy on preventing a war in Asia, Melinda French Gates on the pandemic's toll on women, Ashraf Ghani on Afghanistan's future, CFR's Martin Indyk on the Israeli-Palestinian conflict, CFR's Charles Kupchan and Richard Haass on the case for a new concert of powers, Maya Wang on China's techno-authoritarianism, Michael Woldemariam on toxic politics between the countries of the Nile River basin, and Amos Yadlin and Ebtesam al-Ketbi on the future of the Iran deal.

Clockwise from top left: Foreign Affairs *Editor Daniel Kurtz-Phelan and Vice President and Deputy Director of Studies Shannon K. O'Neil speak with President of the Peterson Institute for International Economics Adam S. Posen and Professor in Urban Policy at Harvard Kennedy School Gordon H. Hanson about their articles in the May/June 2021 issue of* Foreign Affairs.

1921–2021

CELEBRATING A CENTURY

Founded in 1921, the Council on Foreign Relations is an independent, nonpartisan membership organization, think tank, publisher, and educational institution dedicated to informing the public about the foreign policy choices facing the United States and the world. Explore cfr.org/100 and discover the institution's origins and influence in foreign policy over the last one hundred years.

A group of term members is pictured in 1970.

One Hundred Years of Speakers

CFR has hosted hundreds of distinguished guests over the years, including heads of state, thought leaders, and news makers. Learn who said what at CFR by visiting cfr.org/100. Highlights of meetings include Secretary of State Henry L. Stimson's visit in 1932, when he announced what later became known as the Stimson Doctrine, and Prime Minister of Pakistan Imran Khan's visit in 2019, when he discussed the disputed region of Kashmir. Entries include a description of the speaker's remarks, their connection to CFR, and historical photos from the Council's archives.

1932
Henry L. Stimson

1948
George F. Kennan

1956
Harry S. Truman

1966
Indira Gandhi

1979
Dalai Lama

1983
George H.W. Bush

1990
Nelson Mandela

1995
Madeleine Albright

2006
Ellen Johnson Sirleaf

2007
Benazir Bhutto

2018
Justin Trudeau

2019
Imran Khan

Timeline: 1921–2021

A timeline on the website offers a ready survey of important moments that have shaped the institution over the last one hundred years, from the first study groups conducted on postwar economics in 1923, to the launch of the original CFR website in 1997, to the publication of an Independent Task Force report on pandemic preparedness in 2020.

1921

Council on Foreign Relations is founded.

John W. Davis
First President
1921–33

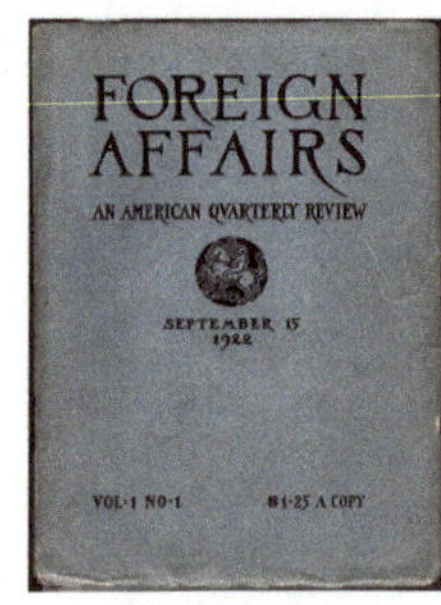

1922

Foreign Affairs publishes its first issue, edited by Archibald Cary Coolidge.

1923

CFR gathers its first study groups, one on Postwar Financial and Economic Problems, and another on Dangerous Areas in Europe.

1925

Malcolm W. Davis is executive director from 1925 to 1927.

1928

CFR begins to publish the *Political Handbook of the World*. Edited by Executive Director Walter H. Mallory, the publication is released annually until 1987.

1930

CFR moves into 45 East 65th Street building, its New York headquarters for the next fifteen years.

1930

CFR publishes *United States in World Affairs* and continues to do so on an annual basis for forty-six years. The publication is then succeeded by the *Foreign Affairs* annual year-end issue titled *America and the World* (1978–93).

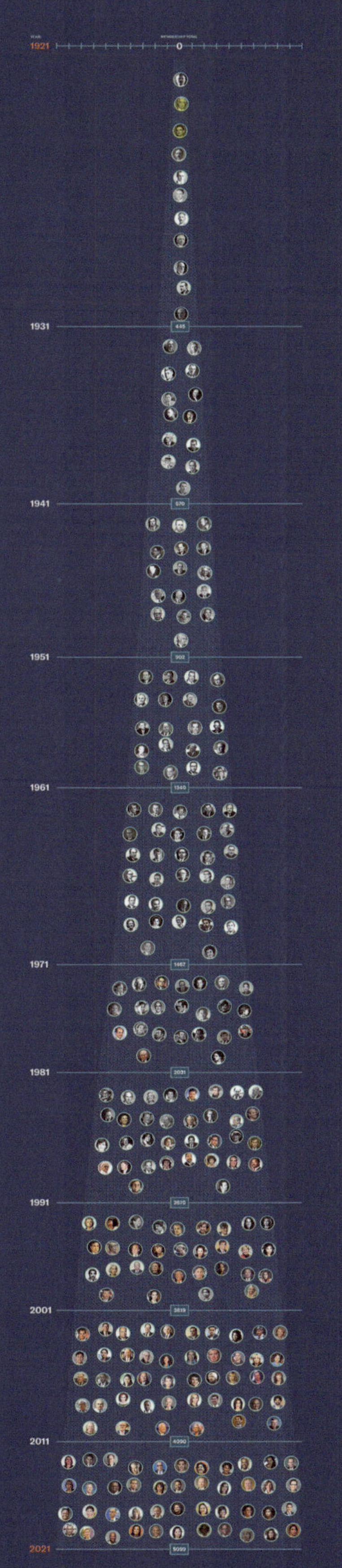

A Changing Membership

Since its founding in 1921, CFR has grown a membership of more than five thousand of the most prominent leaders in the foreign policy arena, including top government officials, scholars, business executives, journalists, lawyers, and nonprofit professionals.

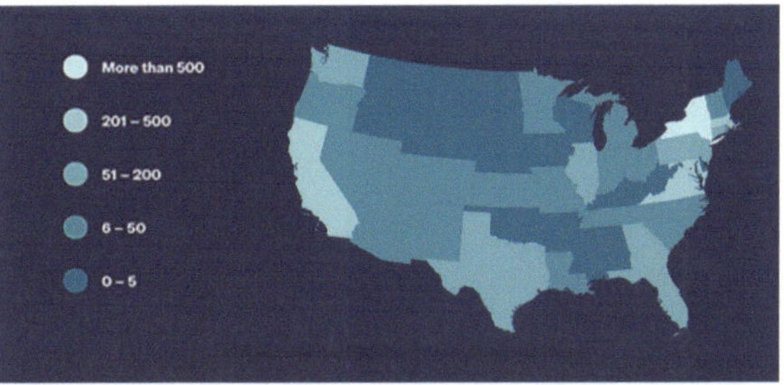

Foreign Affairs: From the Archives

Read twenty-six of the magazine's greatest hits, from George F. Kennan and Henry Kissinger to Samuel P. Huntington and Francis Fukuyama. Articles published prior to 1975 may be accessed with a subscription to *Foreign Affairs*.

Visit cfr.org/100 to learn more.

Membership

Membership

Since its founding in 1921, the Council on Foreign Relations has grown a membership of more than five thousand prominent leaders in the foreign policy arena, including top government officials, scholars, business executives, journalists, lawyers, and nonprofit professionals. The membership is composed of those residing in the greater New York and Washington, DC, areas, and a plurality based around the United States and abroad.

CFR members enjoy unparalleled access to a nonpartisan forum through which they engage with and gain insight from experts in international affairs. Members have in-person access to world leaders, senior government officials, members of Congress, and prominent thinkers and practitioners in academia, policy, and business, many of whom are members themselves. Convening nearly one thousand events annually, CFR is dedicated to facilitating an intellectual exchange of ideas through expert panel discussions, symposia, town halls, livestreams, and CEO forums exclusively for members. Through exposure to CFR's think tank, publications, briefing materials, and special content on CFR.org and ForeignAffairs.com, members benefit from an expansive collection of unmatched intellectual capital and resources.

The Council seeks quality, diversity, and balance in its membership. Criteria for membership include intellectual achievement and expertise; degree of experience, interest, and current involvement in international affairs; promise of future achievement and service in foreign relations; potential contributions to CFR's work; desire and ability to participate in CFR activities; and standing among peers. New members are elected twice a year by the Board of Directors.

Applying for Membership

Eligibility Requirements

- Membership is restricted to U.S. citizens (native born or naturalized) and permanent residents who have applied to become citizens.
- CFR visiting fellows are prohibited from applying for membership until they have completed their fellowship tenure.
- CFR members are required to fulfill annual dues requirements.

Candidates must submit an online application, complete with a nominating letter from a current CFR member and seconding letters from three to four other individuals.

To apply for membership, visit cfr.org/membership/individual-membership.

Membership Deadlines and Candidate Notification

The two annual membership application deadlines are March 1 and November 1. All membership candidates and their letter writers will receive notification of the election decisions in late June for the March 1 deadline, and in early March for the November 1 deadline.

For More Information

To learn more about the membership application process or for information on nominating a candidate, visit cfr.org/membership or contact Membership at 212.434.9456 or applications@cfr.org.

Stephen M. Kellen Term Member Program

The Stephen M. Kellen Term Member Program, established in 1970 to cultivate the next generation of foreign policy leaders, encourages professionals from diverse backgrounds to engage in a sustained conversation on international affairs and U.S. foreign policy. Each year, a new class of term members between the ages of thirty and thirty-six is elected to serve a fixed five-year term. Term members enjoy a full range of activities, including events with high-profile speakers; an annual Term Member Conference; roundtables; trips to various sites, including military bases, international organizations, and U.S. governmental agencies; and one weeklong study trip abroad every two years.

For more information on the Term Member Program, please visit cfr.org/membership/term-member-program.

Applying for Term Membership

Eligibility Requirements

- Term membership is restricted to U.S. citizens (native born or naturalized) and permanent residents who have applied to become citizens.
- Candidates for term membership must be between the ages of thirty and thirty-six on January 1 of the year in which they apply.
- CFR visiting fellows are prohibited from applying for term membership until they have completed their fellowship tenure.
- Graduate students should generally wait until after the completion of their degree to apply for term membership.
- CFR term members are required to fulfill annual dues requirements.

Term membership candidates must submit an online application, complete with a nominating letter from a current CFR member and seconding letters from two to three other individuals.

To apply for term membership, visit cfr.org/membership/individual-membership.

Term Membership Deadline and Candidate Notification

The annual application deadline for term membership is January 3. All term membership candidates and their letter writers will receive notification of the election decisions in late June.

Profile of the Membership

Between July 2020 and June 2021, CFR membership increased by 1 percent, from 5,125 to 5,172 members. Member records are maintained by CFR at 58 East 68th Street, New York, NY 10065.

Location	Number of Members	Percentage of Membership
National	2,143	41
New York Area	1,476	29
Washington, DC, Area	1,553	30
Total	5,172	100

Industry		
Education	1,059	21
Nonprofit	1,006	19
Financial Institutions	774	15
Law and Consulting	670	13
Government	422	8
Media and News Services	320	6
Commerce	171	3
Information Technology	142	3
Military	114	2
Medicine and Health Care	61	1
Energy and Power	37	1
Other	396	8
Total	5,172	100

5,172

individual members

New York City Area	*Washington, DC, Area*	*National*
1,476	**1,553**	**2,143**

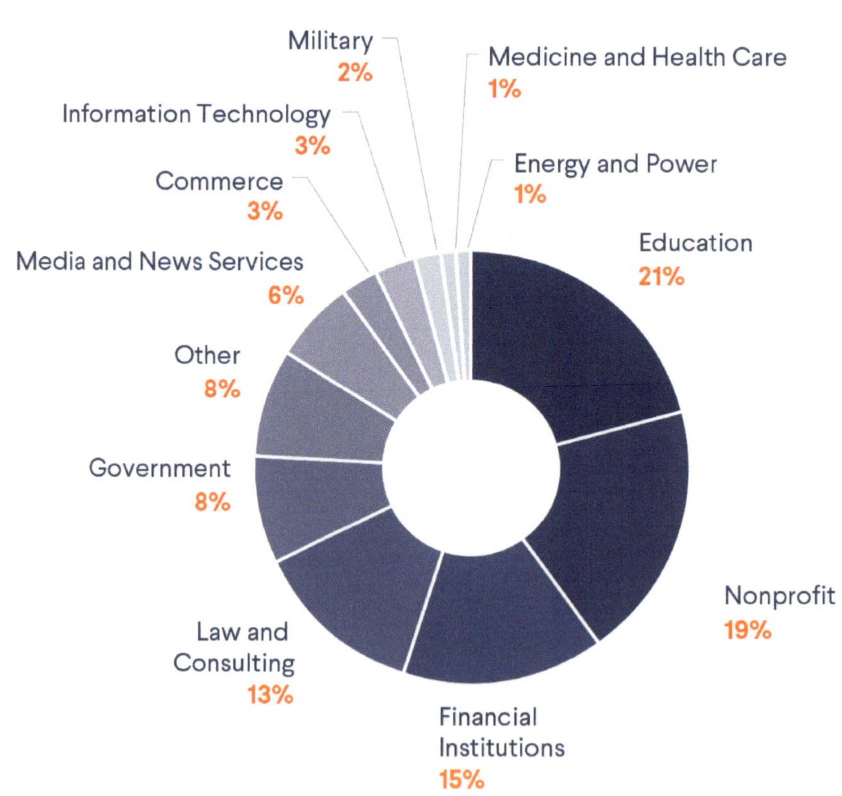

Corporate Program

Profile of the Corporate Membership

Founded in 1953 with twenty-five corporate members, the Corporate Program has since expanded to include more than 120 companies from various industries and regions of the world. Through CFR's unmatched convening power, the program links private-sector leaders with decision-makers from government, media, nongovernmental organizations, and academia to discuss issues at the intersection of business and foreign policy.

Corporate membership is available at three levels: Founders ($100,000), President's Circle ($75,000), and Affiliates ($40,000). Member companies are offered briefings by in-house experts, a members-only website, CFR resources tailored to the private sector, and roundtables designed specifically for executives. The highlight of the program year is the annual Corporate Conference, which addresses such topics as competitiveness, geopolitical risk, and the global economic outlook. Additionally, the program provides professional development opportunities for individuals on a senior management track through its Corporate Leaders Program, and, for those with fewer than ten years of experience, through its Young Professionals Briefing series.

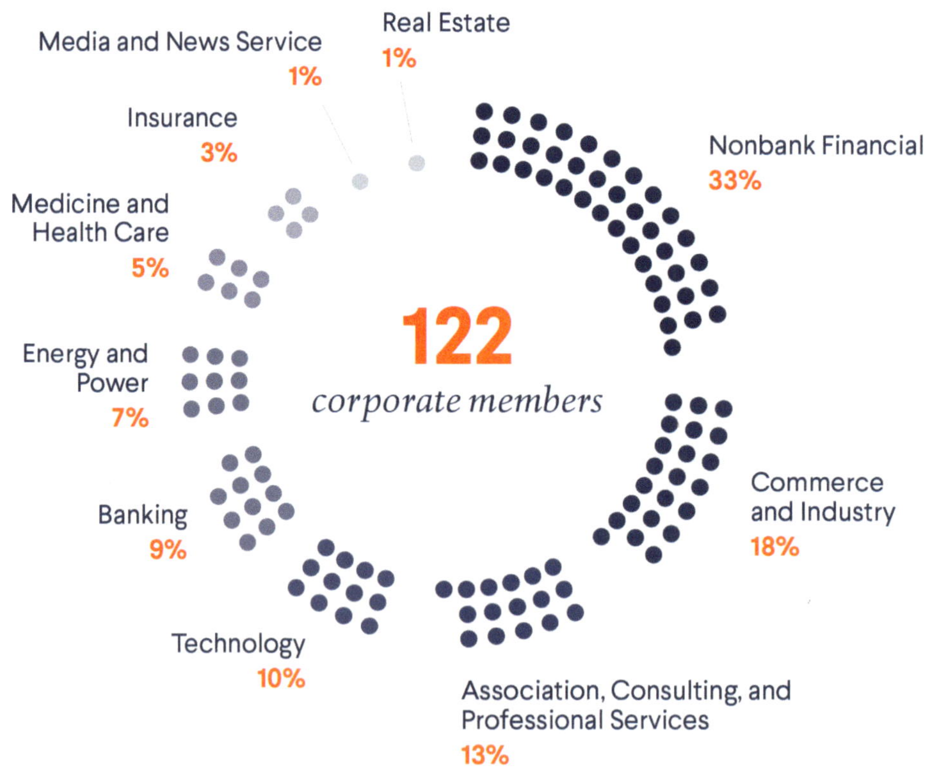

Note: *Percentages do not necessarily total 100 because of rounding.*

Benefits of Corporate Membership

Founders ($100,000+)

All President's Circle and Affiliates benefits plus:

- Four CFR fellow briefings tailored to the company's interests
- Professional development opportunity for four rising executives to participate as "Corporate Leaders" in conjunction with the competitive Stephen M. Kellen Term Member Program
- One rental of the historic Harold Pratt House ballroom and library (based on availability)
- Online site license arrangements and fifteen *Foreign Affairs* print subscriptions
- One-time cover or premium position advertisement in *Foreign Affairs*, with exclusive discounts on digital, sponsored content, and continued print advertising
- Prominent logo placement on the Corporate Program webpage and at the Corporate Conference

President's Circle ($75,000)

All Affiliates benefits plus:

- Invitations for leadership-level executives to attend the Chairman's Circle Dinner and the Annual Dinner with CFR's Board of Directors and Global Board of Advisors
- Opportunities for senior executives to participate in study groups and roundtables led by CFR fellows, and attend exclusive events with noted thinkers and practitioners in government, policy, academia, and the private sector
- Priority registration for meetings, roundtables, and high-level events
- Two CFR fellow briefings tailored to the company's interests
- Professional development opportunity for two rising executives to participate as "Corporate Leaders" in conjunction with the competitive Stephen M. Kellen Term Member Program
- Ten *Foreign Affairs* print subscriptions
- One-time full-page advertisement in *Foreign Affairs*, with exclusive discounts on digital, sponsored content, and continued print advertising

Affiliates ($40,000)

- Invitations for executives to participate in a range of in-person CFR events each year in New York, Washington, DC, and other major cities in the United States and around the world
- Participation in virtual meetings and rapid-response discussions led by CFR fellows and other experts
- Access to meeting replays, CFR resources tailored to the private sector, and other digital resources, including the member services portal
- Opportunities for senior executives to participate in special meetings and roundtables with CFR's president
- Opportunities for young professionals to participate in special briefings and select meetings
- Invitations for executives to attend the Corporate Conference, CFR's annual summit on geopolitical and geoeconomic issues of interest to the global business community
- One CFR fellow briefing tailored to the company's interests
- Reduced rates for rental of the Harold Pratt House in New York City and 1777 F Street in Washington, DC
- Six *Foreign Affairs* print subscriptions
- Exclusive discounts on additional *Foreign Affairs* subscriptions, advertising, and custom events with editors
- Recognition on CFR's corporate membership roster

Note: *Corporate membership dues are 65 percent tax deductible.*
For more information, please contact the Corporate Program at corporate@cfr.org or 212.434.9684.

Financial Highlights

Statement of Financial Position

As of June 30, 2021 (with comparative totals for June 30, 2020)

Assets	2021	2020	Change
Cash and cash equivalents	$ 49,786,200	$ 37,195,600	$ 12,590,600
Accounts receivable, net	1,955,900	2,117,200	(161,300)
Prepaid expenses	1,181,200	1,363,100	(181,900)
Grants and contributions receivable, net	13,088,400	21,935,000	(8,846,600)
Contributions receivable for endowment, net	14,443,000	15,304,600	(861,600)
Inventory	167,200	121,400	45,800
Investments	589,309,500	479,956,700	109,352,800
Land, buildings and building improvements, and equipment, net	62,930,300	66,242,100	(3,311,800)
Total assets	**732,861,700**	**624,235,700**	**108,626,000**
Liabilities			
Accounts payable and accrued expenses	8,989,700	8,087,800	901,900
Deferred revenue	6,251,100	6,183,300	67,800
Accrued postretirement benefits	4,949,000	5,848,000	(899,000)
Interest-rate swap agreement	7,659,100	10,918,900	(3,259,800)
Bonds payable	48,630,000	50,599,100	(1,969,100)
Total liabilities	**76,478,900**	**81,637,100**	**(5,158,200)**
Net assets			
Without donor restrictions	142,857,100	113,484,900	29,372,200
With donor restrictions	513,525,700	429,113,700	84,412,000
Total net assets	**656,382,800**	**542,598,600**	**113,784,200**
Total liabilities and net assets	**$732,861,700**	**$624,235,700**	**$108,626,000**

Note: *To view the full 2021 Financial Statements, please visit cfr.org/annual-report-2021.*

Statement of Activities

For the year ended June 30, 2021

Operating revenue and support	Without donor restrictions	With donor restrictions	Total
Membership dues	$ 8,052,200	$ —	$ 8,052,200
Annual giving	10,605,200	—	10,605,200
Corporate memberships and related income	6,850,000	121,700	6,971,700
Grants and contributions	1,470,500	10,732,500	12,203,000
Foreign Affairs publications	9,298,200	—	9,298,200
Investment return used for current operations	6,895,500	16,098,600	22,994,100
Rental income	151,300	—	151,300
Miscellaneous	73,900	—	73,900
Net assets released from restrictions	27,245,900	(27,245,900)	—
Total operating revenue and support	**70,642,700**	**(293,100)**	**70,349,600**

Operating expenses

Program expenses:			
Studies Program	22,565,700	—	22,565,700
Task Force	446,100	—	446,100
NY Meetings	1,061,600	—	1,061,600
DC programs	1,279,900	—	1,279,900
Special events	600,800	—	600,800
Foreign Affairs publications	9,772,700	—	9,772,700
National Program	885,400	—	885,400
Outreach Program	1,471,000	—	1,471,000
Term member	351,700	—	351,700
Digital Program	5,524,100	—	5,524,100
Education Program	4,898,700	—	4,898,700
Global Board of Advisors	26,800	—	26,800
Total program expenses	**$48,854,500**	**$ –**	**$48,854,500**

Note: *To view the full 2021 Financial Statements, please visit cfr.org/annual-report-2021.*

2021

	Without donor restrictions	With donor restrictions	Total
Supporting services			
Fundraising:			
Development	$ 2,113,600	$ —	$ 2,113,600
Corporate Program	1,741,200	—	1,741,200
Total fundraising	**3,854,800**	**–**	**3,854,800**
Management and general	14,747,200	—	14,747,200
Membership	1,654,200	—	1,654,200
Total supporting services	**20,256,200**	**–**	**20,256,200**
Total operating expenses	**69,110,700**	**–**	**69,110,700**
Transfer from operating to innovation fund for *Foreign Affairs*	(1,000,000)	—	(1,000,000)
Excess (deficiency) of operating revenue and support over operating expenses and transfers	**532,000**	**(293,100)**	**238,900**
Nonoperating activities			
Investment loss in excess of spending rate	23,886,400	76,908,300	100,794,700
Endowment contributions	—	7, 896,800	7, 896,800
Change in value of interest-rate swap agreement	3,259,800	—	3,259,800
Other	(205,000)	(100,000)	(305,000)
Postretirement changes other than net periodic costs	899,000	—	899,000
Transfer from operating to innovation fund for *Foreign Affairs*	1,000,000	—	1,000,000
Total nonoperating activities	**28,840,200**	**84,705,100**	**113,545,300**
Change in net assets	**29,372,200**	**84,412,000**	**113,784,200**
Net assets, beginning of year	**113,484,900**	**429,113,700**	**542,598,600**
Net assets, end of year	**$142,857,100**	**$513,525,700**	**$656,382,800**

Note: *To view the full 2021 Financial Statements, please visit cfr.org/annual-report-2021.*

Statement of Activities

For the year ended June 30, 2020

Operating revenue and support	Without donor restrictions	With donor restrictions	Total
Membership dues	$ 7,708,800	$ —	$ 7,708,800
Annual giving	9,736,900	—	9,736,900
Corporate memberships and related income	6,678,000	217,000	6,895,000
Grants and contributions	1,685,800	16,317,400	18,003,200
Foreign Affairs publications	8,650,100	—	8,650,100
Investment return used for current operations	5,929,900	16,016,200	21,946,100
Rental income	1,204,000	—	1,204,000
Miscellaneous	326,800	1,500	328,300
Net assets released from restrictions	34,023,900	(34,023,900)	—
Total operating revenue and support	**75,944,200**	**(1,471,800)**	**74,472,400**

Operating expenses			
Program expenses:			
Studies Program	24,243,300	—	24,243,300
Task Force	326,000	—	326,000
NY Meetings	1,392,100	—	1,392,100
DC programs	1,605,400	—	1,605,400
Special events	796,000	—	796,000
Foreign Affairs	10,569,200	—	10,569,200
National Program	1,183,100	—	1,183,100
Outreach Program	1,864,900	—	1,864,900
Term member	494,900	—	494,900
Digital Program	6,198,900	—	6,198,900
Education Program	4,539,100	—	4,539,100
Global Board of Advisors	88,100	—	88,100
Total program expenses	**$53,301,000**	**$ –**	**$53,301,000**

Note: *To view the full 2021 Financial Statements, please visit cfr.org/annual-report-2021.*

2020

	Without donor restrictions	With donor restrictions	Total
Supporting services			
Fundraising:			
Development	$ 2,382,000	$ —	$ 2,382,000
Corporate Program	2,090,400	—	2,090,400
Total fundraising	**4,472,400**	**–**	**4,472,400**
Management and general	16,284,300	—	16,284,300
Membership	1,660,100	—	1,660,100
Total supporting services	**22,416,800**	**–**	**22,416,800**
Total operating expenses	**75,717,800**	**–**	**75,717,800**
Excess (deficiency) of operating revenue and support over operating expenses	**226,400**	**(1,471,800)**	**(1,245,400)**
Nonoperating activities			
Investment loss in excess of spending rate	(2,101,800)	(4,753,400)	(6,855,200)
Endowment contributions	2,360,000	6,521,200	8,881,200
Change in value of interest-rate swap agreement	(4,006,700)	—	(4,006,700)
Other	(5,300)	(219,700)	(225,000)
Postretirement changes other than net periodic costs	22,000	—	22,000
Total nonoperating activities	**(3,731,800)**	**1,548,100**	**(2,183,700)**
Change in net assets	**(3,505,400)**	**76,300**	**(3,429,100)**
Net assets, beginning of year	**116,990,300**	**429,037,400**	**546,027,700**
Net assets, end of year	**$113,484,900**	**$429,113,700**	**$542,598,600**

Note: *To view the full 2021 Financial Statements, please visit cfr.org/annual-report-2021.*

Credits

Editor: Patricia Lee Dorff
Associate Editors: Katherine De Chant and Hunter Hallman
Staff Editor: Cassandra Jensen
Photo Editor: Hunter Hallman
Copy Editor: Glenn Court
Cover Design: Sabine Baumgartner and Dalia Albarran Palma
Production: Gene Crofts
Publications Intern: Mia DiFelice

Photos

Page 23: Suparna Chaudhry

Page 30, bottom: Council on Foreign Relations

Page 30–31, top: *Prime Minister Georges Clemenceau of France spoke at CFR's first marquee event in November 1921. He was accompanied by a number of U.S. dignitaries, including diplomat and Managing Editor of* Foreign Affairs *magazine Hamilton Fish Armstrong.* (Museum of the City of New York)

Page 31, top row: Library of Congress; Eric Schwab/Hulton Archive/Getty Images; Council on Foreign Relations; Consolidated News Pictures/Getty Images

Page 31, middle row: Council on Foreign Relations

Page 31, bottom row: Kaveh Sardari/www.sardari.com; Council on Foreign Relations; Don Pollard; Don Pollard

www.ingramcontent.com/pod-product-compliance
Lightning Source LLC
LaVergne TN
LVHW070222110826
845147LV00003B/620

* 9 7 8 0 8 7 6 0 9 3 9 5 5 *